W9-CDV-691

What's in Your Body?

by Ximena Hastings
illustrations by Alison Hawkins

Ready-to-Read

SIMON SPOTLIGHT
An imprint of Simon & Schuster Children's Publishing Division
New York   London   Toronto   Sydney   New Delhi
1230 Avenue of the Americas, New York, New York 10020
This Simon Spotlight edition December 2022
Text copyright © 2022 by Simon & Schuster, Inc.
Illustrations copyright © 2022 by Alison Hawkins • Stock photos by iStock
All rights reserved, including the right of reproduction in whole or in part in any form.
SIMON SPOTLIGHT, READY-TO-READ, and colophon are registered trademarks of Simon & Schuster, Inc.
For information about special discounts for bulk purchases, please contact Simon & Schuster Special Sales at
1-866-506-1949 or business@simonandschuster.com.
Manufactured in the United States of America 1022 LAK
2 4 6 8 10 9 7 5 3 1
Cataloging-in-Publication Data for this title is available from the Library of Congress.
ISBN 978-1-6659-2790-1 (hc) • ISBN 978-1-6659-2789-5 (pbk) • ISBN 978-1-6659-2791-8 (ebook)

Glossary

bacteria: microorganisms that live in the body

bladder: a sack in the body that temporarily holds urine

blood cells: small biological units found within blood

blood vessels: tubes that carry blood through the body

germs: tiny organisms that cause disease

infection: what happens when germs get inside the body, causing illness

intestines: the large and small intestines are part of the digestive tract that extends from the stomach to remove solid waste from the body

mucus: a slippery fluid that moistens and protects different parts of the body

organ: a body part that performs a specific function

pus: a liquid formed as a result of an infection and is made up of dead white blood cells, broken-down body tissue, and germs

Note to readers: Some of these words may have more than one definition. The definitions above match how these words are used in this book.

Contents

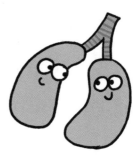

Chapter 1: What's Under Your Skin?

Hello! My name is Dr. Ick, and this is my friend, Sam. We like to study things that are sticky, icky, and disgusting!

In our years of studying,
we have never come across
anything more gross than . . .
THE HUMAN BODY!

There are a lot of yucky, fun facts we know about the body! For example, do you know which long, slippery tube moves all the food and drink in our bodies?

It's the **intestines** (say: in-TEH-stuhns). Everything we eat gets digested, or broken down, in the large and small intestines so that our bodies get the fuel they need. When stretched out, the large intestine can measure up to five feet long. But the small intestine can measure up to twenty-five feet long!

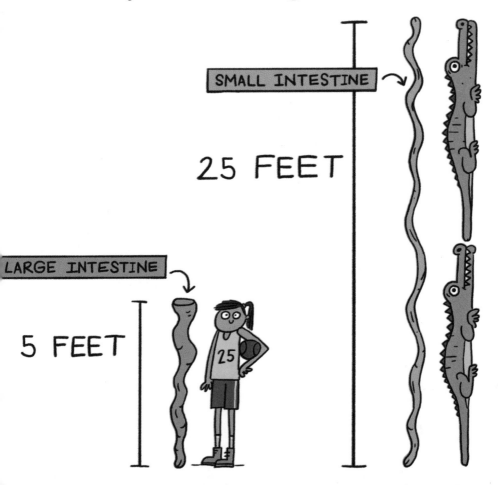

SMALL INTESTINE

25 FEET

LARGE INTESTINE

5 FEET

25

Do you know what the biggest **organ** in the body is?
The skin!

The skin is an organ?

Yes! And it does a lot of work.
The skin can shed up to
two hundred million skin cells
every single hour!

Our blood is located underneath
our skin.
It travels through long, skinny tubes
called veins (say: VAYNS).

Veins are **blood vessels** that carry
blood from different parts of our
bodies to our heart.
They can stretch out more than sixty
thousand miles.
That would circle the Earth almost
two-and-a-half times!

Chapter 2:
Boogey, Oogey, Boogers!

Next let's get to some more gross stuff
in the human body . . . BOOGERS,
or dried **mucus.**
Boogers don't only form in our noses.
Did you know we even get boogers
in our eyes?

This is called eye crust, and it forms in our eyes when we sleep because we aren't blinking away our normal eye mucus. This means the mucus builds up and turns into a sticky crust.

Did you know there are tiny
bugs near our eyes too?

What is
THAT?

Some eyelashes carry bugs
called mites!
That might sound scary, but
mites have an important job to do!
They help clean up dead skin, mucus,
and skin oils around our eyes.

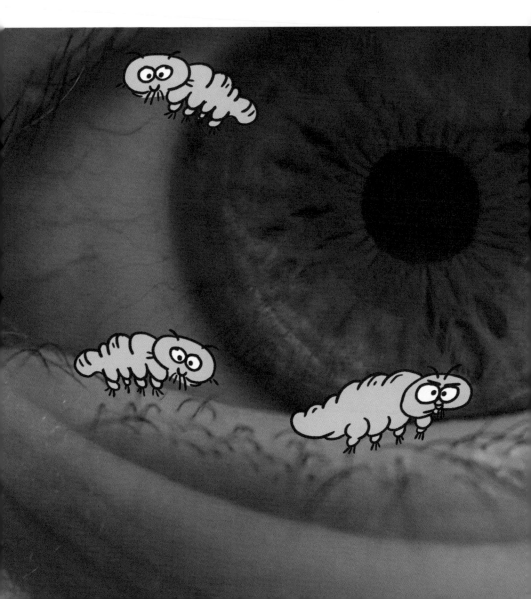

Let's talk about one of my
very favorite gross things: **pus**!

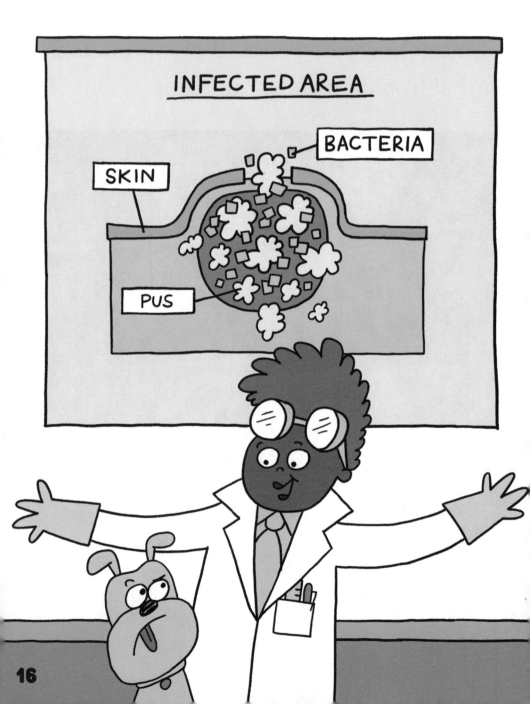

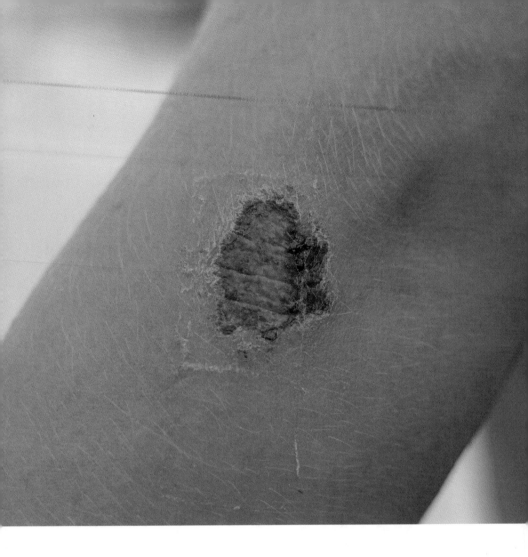

Pus is made up of a liquid of dead **blood cells**. When pus forms, it is a sign that your body has an **infection**.

Now let's move on to **germs**.
Our hands alone can carry more
than three thousand different
kinds of germs!
Germs can move around easily from
one person's skin to another person's.
Even giving someone a high five
can transfer lots of germs!

That is why it is so important
to wash your hands.

Chapter 3: The Scoop on Pee and Poop!

Now I want to tell you about something super gross and stinky—pee and poop!

Pee and poop are gross,
but they are important.
They help get all the waste out
of the body.

Pee, or urine, is a yellow liquid
that is stored in the **bladder**.
It is made up of waste and water.
When your bladder is full,
your body tells you it's time to pee!

Bladders can hold around six hundred
milliliters of liquid.
That's about the size
of a pint of ice cream!

Feces (say: FEE-seas), or poop,
is also made up of waste
from your body.
Poop smells because it
contains a lot more **bacteria**
than urine does.

Bacteria help break down the food
in our bodies.
But as they do, they leave
a stinky smell behind!

Have you ever noticed
different-colored feces?

The color of your poop can
tell you how your body is feeling!

BROWN
You are
feeling fine!

GREEN
You might have
had a lot of veggies
or green foods.

YELLOW
You might have
had too much
fatty food.

Sometimes bacteria have a hard time breaking down the food we eat. When this happens, gas starts to develop in our bodies, and it gets released.

It makes a loud sound and can be very stinky.

Passing gas may be stinky,
but it's important that you don't
hold it in!
When you do, the gas in your body can
travel upward and come out through
your mouth.
That's when you burp!

Isn't it amazing how many gross things human bodies can do?

We'll talk about the things in dogs'
bodies another time.
There's lots of cool and icky stuff in
them, too!
But even though our bodies are
stinky and slimy, they
work hard to keep us happy
and healthy!

Make Your Own Skeleton!

Before starting this activity, make sure to
ask a grown-up for help!

You will need:

- craft glue
- 20 craft sticks
- tape
- pasta (different shapes like macaroni, spaghetti, shells, and spirals)
- a picture of a skeletal system (ask a grown-up to help you look online, or look one up in a book!)

Directions:

- Arrange twenty craft sticks in a row from top to bottom and tape them together on the back.
- Then grab four pieces of macaroni pasta and glue them onto the very top of your craft sticks to make the head.
- Next, add three spirals and arrange them in a line to make the human spine.
- Next, add four pieces of macaroni next to the spirals to make the lungs.
- Now add two shells to the bottom of the spine to create the hips.
- Use spaghetti to make the arms, legs, hands, and feet. (You might have to break a few pieces in half!)
- Let the glue dry overnight, and wake up to find your very own skeleton!